Passionfood

100 LOVE POEMS FOR THOSE IN LOVE

Passionfood is more than a feast of poetry. It's a celebration of true love – love that grows into love that lasts, love that fills every part of our lives, love that never leaves us.

Its menu is distinctively different from that of other anthologies of love poetry. There are no broken hearts here.

Compiled by *Staying Alive* editor Neil Astley, *Passionfood* opens with poems about attraction, desire and longing. The next two sections cover the excitement of love, with many passionate poems about being and staying in love. Finally, there are the fruits of deepening love: poems celebrating closeness, trust and mutual understanding, poems of joy, wisdom and shared recognition.

Passionfood is a book of positive, provocative and witty love poems for everyone whose life has been nourished and sustained by love, mixing passion with food for thought. It's also a book which holds out hope, and as such, a perfect gift for the person you love, for weddings and engagements, birthdays and anniversaries.

D0094225

For Pamela

Passionfood

100 LOVE POEMS

EDITED BY NEIL ASTLEY

BLOODAXE BOOKS

Selection copyright © 2005 Neil Astley.

Copyright of poems rests with authors and other rights holders as cited in the acknowledgements on pages 126-28, which constitute an extension of this copyright page.

ISBN: 1 85224 727 4

First published 2005 by
Bloodaxe Books Ltd,
Highgreen,
Tarset,
Northumberland NE48 1RP.

www.bloodaxebooks.com
For further information about Bloodaxe titles
please visit our website or write to
the above address for a catalogue.

Bloodaxe Books Ltd acknowledges
the financial assistance of
Arts Council England, North East.

LEGAL NOTICE
All rights reserved. No part of this book may be reproduced, stored in a retrieval system, or transmitted in any form, or by any means, electronic, mechanical, photocopying, recording or otherwise, without prior written permission from the copyright holders listed on pages 126-28. Bloodaxe Books Ltd only controls publication rights to poems from its own publications and does *not* control rights to most of the poems published in this anthology.

Printed in Great Britain by Cromwell Press Ltd, Trowbridge, Wiltshire.

Contents

3. DESSERT

1.

DESIRE

(*APPETISERS*)

The first course of *Passionfood* is a selection of tantalising poems about desire, sexual attraction and longing, beginning with two love sonnets.

The opening sonnet (10) is from Pablo Neruda's *100 Love Sonnets*, a book of a hundred poems all written for his beloved wife Matilde (there's another on page 104). The second sonnet (11) is by American poet Marilyn Hacker from *Love, Death, and the Changing of the Seasons*, her book-length sonnet sequence telling the story of a love affair between two women.

Sonnets have always been a popular form in love poetry. This anthology includes four of the 154 sonnets (16, 60, 61, 112) written by Shakespeare during the 1590s. Shakespeare's sonnets have been the subject of much scholarly and biographical speculation, some being addressed to a mistress or 'Dark Lady' but many more to a young man, possibly the Earl of Southampton.

FROM

100 Love Sonnets

PABLO NERUDA
(Chile, 1904-73)

translated from the Spanish
by STEPHEN TAPSCOTT

I crave your mouth, your voice, your hair.
Silent and starving, I prowl through the streets.
Bread does not nourish me, dawn disrupts me, all day
I hunt for the liquid measure of your steps.

I hunger for your sleek laugh,
your hands the color of a savage harvest,
hunger for the pale stones of your fingernails,
I want to eat your skin like a whole almond.

I want to eat the sunbeam flaring in your lovely body,
the sovereign nose of your arrogant face,
I want to eat the fleeting shade of your lashes,

and I pace around hungry, sniffing the twilight,
hunting for you, for your hot heart,
like a puma in the barrens of Quitratúe.

'O little one…'

MARILYN HACKER
(USA, *b.* 1942)

O little one, this longing is the pits.
I'm horny as a timber wolf in heat.
Three times a night, I tangle up the sheet.
I seem to flirt with everything with tits:
Karyn at lunch, who knows I think she's cute;
my ex, the D.A. on the Sex Crimes Squad;
Iva's gnarled, canny New England god-
mother, who was my Saturday night date.
I'm trying to take things one at a time:
situps at bedtime, less coffee, less meat,
more showers, till a remedy appears.
Since there's already quite enough Sex Crime,
I think I ought to be kept off the street.
What are you doing for the next five years?

Barefoot

ANNE SEXTON
(USA, 1928-74)

Loving me with my shoes off
means loving my long brown legs,
sweet dears, as good as spoons;
and my feet, those two children
let out to play naked. Intricate nubs,
my toes. No longer bound.
And what's more, see toenails and
prehensile joints of joints and
all ten stages, root by root.
All spirited and wild, this little
piggy went to market and this little piggy
stayed. Long brown legs and long brown toes.
Further up, my darling, the woman
is calling her secrets, little houses,
little tongues that tell you.

There is no one else but us
in this house on the land spit.
The sea wears a bell in its navel.
And I'm your barefoot wench for a
whole week. Do you care for salami?
No. You'd rather not have a scotch?
No. You don't really drink. You do
drink me. The gulls kill fish,
crying out like three-year-olds.
The surf's a narcotic, calling out,
I am, I am, I am
all night long. Barefoot,
I drum up and down your back.

In the morning I run from door to door
of the cabin playing *chase me.*
Now you grab me by the ankles.
Now you work your way up the legs
and come to pierce me at my hunger mark.

For Desire

KIM ADDONIZIO
(USA, *b.* 1954)

Give me the strongest cheese, the one that stinks best;
and I want the good wine, the swirl in crystal
surrendering the bruised scent of blackberries,
or cherries, the rich spurt in the back
of the throat, the holding it there before swallowing.
Give me the lover who yanks open the door
of his house and presses me to the wall
in the dim hallway, and keeps me there until I'm drenched
and shaking, whose kisses arrive by the boatload
and begin their delicious diaspora
through the cities and small towns of my body.
To hell with the saints, with the martyrs
of my childhood meant to instruct me
in the power of endurance and faith,

to hell with the next world and its pallid angels
swooning and sighing like Victorian girls.
I want this world. I want to walk into
the ocean and feel it trying to drag me along
like I'm nothing but a broken bit of scratched glass,
and I want to resist it. I want to go
staggering and flailing my way
through the bars and back rooms,
through the gleaming hotels and the weedy
lots of abandoned sunflowers and the parks
where dogs are let off their leashes
in spite of the signs, where they sniff each
other and roll together in the grass, I want to
lie down somewhere and suffer for love until
it nearly kills me, and then I want to get up again
and put on that little black dress and wait
for you, yes you, to come over here
and get down on your knees and tell me
just how fucking good I look.

Wild Nights

Wild Nights – Wild Nights!
Were I with thee
Wild Nights should be
Our luxury!

EMILY DICKINSON

(U

ss –

night –

The Sun Rising

JOHN DONNE

(England, 1572-1631)

Busy old fool, unruly sun,
Why dost thou thus,
Through windows, and through curtains, call on us?
Must to thy motions lovers' seasons run?
Saucy pedantic wretch, go chide
Late schoolboys, and sour prentices,
Go tell court-huntsmen, that the King will ride,
Call country ants to harvest offices;
Love, all alike, no season knows, nor clime,
Nor hours, days, months, which are the rags of time.

Thy beams, so reverend, and strong
Why shouldst thou think?
I could eclipse and cloud them with a wink,
But that I would not lose her sight so long:
If her eyes have not blinded thine,
Look, and tomorrow late, tell me,
Whether both th'Indias of spice and mine
Be where thou left'st them, or lie here with me.
Ask for those kings whom thou saw'st yesterday,
And thou shalt hear, All here in one bed lay.

She'is all states, and all princes I,
Nothing else is.
Princes do but play us; compared to this,
All honour's mimic; all wealth alchemy.
Thou sun art half as happy as we,
In that the world's contracted thus;
Thine age asks ease, and since thy duties be
To warm the world, that's done in warming us.
Shine here to us, and thou art everywhere;
This bed thy centre is, these walls, thy sphere.

'So are you to my thoughts as food to life...'

WILLIAM SHAKESPEARE

(England, 1564-1616)

So are you to my thoughts as food to life,
Or as sweet-seasoned showers are to the ground;
And for the peace of you I hold such strife
As 'twixt a miser and his wealth is found.
Now proud as an enjoyer, and anon
Doubting the filching age will steal his treasure,
Now counting best to be with you alone,
Then bettered that the world may see my pleasure,
Sometime all full with feasting on your sight,
And by and by clean starvéd for a look,
Possessing or pursuing no delight
Save what is had, or must from you be took.
  Thus do I pine and surfeit day by day,
  Or gluttoning on all, or all away

'It seems to me that man is equal to the gods'

SAPPHO

(Greece, 7th century BC)

translated from the Greek
by JOSEPHINE BALMER

It seems to me that man is equal to the gods,
that is, whoever sits opposite you
and, drawing nearer, savours, as you speak,
the sweetness of your voice

and the thrill of your laugh, which have so stirred the heart
in my own breast, that whenever I catch
sight of you, even if for a moment,
then my voice deserts me

and my tongue is struck silent, a delicate fire
suddenly races underneath my skin,
my eyes see nothing, my ears whistle like
the whirling of a top

and sweat pours down me and a trembling creeps over
my whole body, I am greener than grass;
at such times, I seem to be no more than
a step away from death;

but all can be endured since even a pauper...

Warming Her Pearls

CAROL ANN DUFFY

(Scotland, *b.* 1955)

Next to my own skin, her pearls. My mistress
bids me wear them, warm them, until evening
when I'll brush her hair. At six, I place them
round her cool, white throat. All day I think of her,

resting in the Yellow Room, contemplating silk
or taffeta, which gown tonight? She fans herself
whilst I work willingly, my slow heat entering
each pearl. Slack on my neck, her rope.

She's beautiful. I dream about her
in my attic bed; picture her dancing
with tall men, puzzled by my faint, persistent scent
beneath her French perfume, her milky stones.

I dust her shoulders with a rabbit's foot,
watch the soft blush seep through her skin
like an indolent sigh. In her looking-glass
my red lips part as though I want to speak.

Full moon. Her carriage brings her home. I see
her every movement in my head...Undressing,
taking off her jewels, her slim hand reaching
for the case, slipping naked into bed, the way

she always does...And I lie here awake,
knowing the pearls are cooling even now
in the room where my mistress sleeps. All night
I feel their absence and I burn.

The Bandaged Shoulder

C. P. CAVAFY
(Egypt, 1863-1933)

translated from the Greek
by EDMUND KEELEY
& PHILLIP SHERRARD

He said he'd hurt himself against a wall or had fallen down.
But there was probably some other reason
for the wounded, the bandaged shoulder.

With a rather abrupt gesture,
reaching for a shelf to bring down
some photographs he wanted to look at,
the bandage came undone and a little blood ran.

I did it up again, taking my time
over the binding; he wasn't in pain
and I liked looking at the blood.
It was a thing of my love, that blood.

When he left, I found, in front of his chair,
a bloody rag, part of the dressing,
a rag to be thrown straight into the garbage;
and I put it to my lips
and kept it there a long while –
the blood of love against my lips.

In Paris with You

JAMES FENTON
(England, *b.* 1949)

Don't talk to me of love. I've had an earful
And I get tearful when I've downed a drink or two.
I'm one of your talking wounded.
I'm a hostage. I'm maroonded.
But I'm in Paris with you.

Yes I'm angry at the way I've been bamboozled
And resentful at the mess that I've been through.
I admit I'm on the rebound
And I don't care where are *we* bound.
I'm in Paris with you.

Do you mind if we do *not* go to the Louvre,
If we say sod off to sodding Notre Dame,
If we skip the Champs Elysées
And remain here in this sleazy
Old hotel room
Doing this and that
To what and whom
Learning who you are,
Learning what I am.

Don't talk to me of love. Let's talk of Paris,
The little bit of Paris in our view.
There's that crack across the ceiling
And the hotel walls are peeling
And I'm in Paris with you.

Don't talk to me of love. Let's talk of Paris.
I'm in Paris with the slightest thing you do.
I'm in Paris with your eyes, your mouth,
I'm in Paris with... all points south.
Am I embarrassing you?
I'm in Paris with you.

Desire

Where true Love burns Desire is Love's pure flame;
It is the reflex of our earthly frame,
That takes its meaning from the nobler part,
And but translates the language of the heart.

SAMUEL TAYLOR COLERIDGE
(England, 1772-1834)

Desire's a Desire

SELIMA HILL
(England, *b.* 1945)

It taunts me
like the muzzle of a gun;
it sinks into my soul like chilled honey
packed into the depths of treacherous wounds;
it wraps me up in cold green sheets
like Indian squaws
who wrap their babies in the soft green sheathes of irises
that smell of starch;
it tattooes my shins;
it itches my thighs
like rampant vaginal flora;
it tickles my cheeks
like silkworms munching mulberry leaves
on silk farms;
it nuzzles my plucked armpits like fat dogs;
it plays me
like a piano being played
by regimented fingers
through pressed sheets;
it walks across my back
like geese at dawn,
or the gentle manners
of my only nurse,
who handles me like glass, or Bethlehem.

My skin is white.
I neither eat nor sleep.
My only desire's a desire
to be free from desire.

You Don't Know What Love Is

KIM ADDONIZIO
(USA, *b.* 1954)

but you know how to raise it in me
like a dead girl winched up from a river. How to
wash off the sludge, the stench of our past.
How to start clean. This love even sits up
and blinks; amazed, she takes a few shaky steps.
Any day now she'll try to eat solid food. She'll want
to get into a fast car, one low to the ground, and drive
to some cinderblock shithole in the desert
where she can drink and get sick and then
dance in nothing but her underwear. You know
where she's headed, you know she'll wake up
with an ache she can't locate and no money
and a terrible thirst. So to hell
with your warm hands sliding inside my shirt
and your tongue down my throat
like an oxygen tube. Cover me
in black plastic. Let the mourners through.

2.

PASSION

(MAIN COURSE)

Passionfood's main course is a wide selection of hearty poems celebrating love: the excitement of love as well as the nature of love, being in love and staying in love.

This section includes poems (32 & 33) by two famous poet-lovers, Elizabeth Barrett Browning and Robert Browning, who eloped to be married in 1846 and afterwards lived in Italy. The anthology includes two of Elizabeth Barrett Browning's *Sonnets from the Portuguese* (32, XLIII; 102, XIV), all of which were written during their courtship.

Lord Byron had many lovers, including his half-sister Augusta, but his best-known love poem, 'She Walks in Beauty' (45), was written after first meeting his cousin, 'the beautiful Mrs Wilmot', wearing a mourning dress of spangled black.

The Roman poet Catullus had an even more scurrilous reputation. His teasing mistress has been identified as Clodia Metelli, an infamous socialite, but the 'Lesbia' addressed in his poems may be a literary name for all the women in his life. Robert Herrick's 'Julia' (51 & 92) is probably a similar *nom d'amour*. The Catullus poem (47) is one of many love poems written on the theme of *carpe diem* (seize the day), which usually means: make love now because life is short and tomorrow we may be dead. Another is Andrew Marvell's 'To His Coy Mistress' (48).

'O tell me the truth about love'

W.H. AUDEN

(England, 1907-73)

Some say that love's a little boy,
　　　　And some say it's a bird,
Some say it makes the world go round,
　　　　And some say that's absurd,
And when I asked the man next-door,
　　　　Who looked as if he knew,
His wife got very cross indeed,
　　　　And said it wouldn't do.

　　Does it look like a pair of pyjamas,
　　　Or the ham in a temperance hotel?
　　Does its odour remind one of llamas,
　　　Or has it a comforting smell?
　　Is it prickly to touch as a hedge is,
　　　Or soft as eiderdown fluff
　　Is it sharp or quite smooth at the edges?
　　　O tell me the truth about love.

Our history books refer to it
　　　　In cryptic little notes,
It's quite a common topic on
　　　　The Transatlantic boats;
I've found the subject mentioned in
　　　　Accounts of suicides,
And even seen it scribbled on
　　　　The backs of railway-guides.

　　Does it howl like a hungry Alsatian,
　　　Or boom like a military band?
　　Could one give a first-rate imitation
　　　On a saw or a Steinway Grand?

Is its singing at parties a riot?
  Does it only like Classical stuff?
Will it stop when one wants to be quiet?
  O tell me the truth about love.

I looked inside the summer-house;
        It wasn't ever there:
I tried the Thames at Maidenhead,
        And Brighton's bracing air.
I don't know what the blackbird sang,
        Or what the tulip said;
But it wasn't in the chicken-run,
        Or underneath the bed.

Can it pull extraordinary faces?
  Is it usually sick on a swing?
Does it spend all its time at the races,
  Or fiddling with pieces of string?
Has it views of its own about money?
  Does it think Patriotism enough?
Are its stories vulgar but funny?
  O tell me the truth about love.

When it comes, will it come without warning
  Just as I'm picking my nose?
Will it knock on my door in the morning,
  Or tread in the bus on my toes?
Will it come like a change in the weather?
  Will its greeting be courteous or rough?
Will it alter my life altogether?
  O tell me the truth about love.

The Great Fires

JACK GILBERT
(USA, *b.* 1925)

Love is apart from all things
Desire and excitement are nothing beside it.
It is not the body that finds love.
What leads us there is the body.
What is not love provokes it.
What is not love quenches it.
Love lays hold of everything we know.
The passions which are called love
also change everything to a newness
at first. Passion is clearly the path
but does not bring us to love.
It opens the castle of our spirit
so that we might find the love which is
a mystery hidden there.
Love is one of many great fires.
Passion is a fire made of many woods,
each of which gives off its special odor
so we can know the many kinds
that are not love. Passion is the paper
and twigs that kindle the flames
but cannot sustain them. Desire perishes
because it tries to be love.
Love is eaten away by appetite.
Love does not last, but it is different
from the passions that do not last.
Love lasts by not lasting.
Isaiah said each man walks in his own fire
for his sins. Love allows us to walk
in the sweet music of our particular heart.

He Wishes for the Cloths of Heaven

W. B. YEATS

(Ireland, 1865-1939)

Had I the heavens' embroidered cloths,
Enwrought with golden and silver light,
The blue and the dim and the dark cloths
Of night and light and the half-light,
I would spread the cloths under your feet:
But I, being poor, have only my dreams;
I have spread my dreams under your feet;
Tread softly because you tread on my dreams.

It's Platonic

RITA ANN HIGGINS

(Ireland, *b.* 1955)

Platonic my eye,

I yearn
for the fullness
of your tongue
making me
burst forth
pleasure after pleasure
after dark,

soaking all my dreams.

FROM

Epipsychidion

PERCY BYSSHE SHELLEY

(England, 1792-1822)

Our breath shall intermix, our bosoms bound,
And our veins beat together; and our lips,
With other eloquence than words, eclipse
The soul that burns between them; and the wells
Which boil under our being's inmost cells,
The fountains of our deepest life, shall be
Confused in Passion's golden purity,
As mountain springs under the morning sun.
We shall become the same, we shall be one
Spirit within two frames, oh! wherefore two?
One passion in twin-hearts, which grows and grew,
Till like two meteors of expanding flame,
Those spheres instinct with it become the same,
Touch, mingle, are transfigured; ever still
Burning, yet ever inconsumable;
In one another's substance finding food,
Like flames too pure and light and unimbued
To nourish their bright lives with baser prey,
Which point to Heaven and cannot pass away:
One hope within two wills, one will beneath
Two overshadowing minds, one life, one death.
One Heaven, one Hell, one immortality,
And one annihilation!

Like That

KIM ADDONIZIO
(USA, *b.* 1954)

Love me like a wrong turn on a bad road late at night, with no moon
and no town anywhere
and a large hungry animal moving heavily through the brush in the ditch.
Love me with a blindfold over your eyes and the sound of rusty water
blurting from the faucet in the kitchen, leaking down through
the floorboards to hot cement. Do it without asking,
without wondering or thinking anything, while the machinery's
shut down and the watchman's slumped asleep before his small TV
showing the empty garage, the deserted hallways, while the thieves slice
through
the fence with steel clippers. Love me when you can't find
a decent restaurant open anywhere, when you're alone in a glaring diner
with two nuns arguing in the back booth, when your eggs are greasy
and your hash browns underdone. Snick the buttons off the front of my dress
and toss them one by one into the pond where carp lurk just beneath
the surface,
their cold fins waving. Love me on the hood of a truck no one's driven
in years, sunk to its fenders in weeds and dead sunflowers;
and in the lilies, your mouth on my white throat, while turtles drag
their bellies through slick mud, through the footprints of coots and ducks.
Do it when no one's looking, when the riots begin and the planes open up,
when the bus leaps the curb and the driver hits the brakes and the pedal
sinks to the floor,
while someone hurls a plate against the wall and picks up another,
love me like a freezing shot of vodka, like pure agave, love me
when you're lonely, when we're both too tired to speak, when you don't believe
in anything, listen, there isn't anything, it doesn't matter; lie down
with me and close your eyes, the road curves here, I'm cranking up the radio
and we're going, we won't turn back as long as you love me,
as long as you keep on doing it exactly like that.

'How do I love thee?'

ELIZABETH BARRETT BROWNING

(England, 1806-61)

How do I love thee? Let me count the ways.
I love thee to the depth and breadth and height
My soul can reach, when feeling out of sight
For the ends of Being and Ideal Grace.
I love thee to the level of everyday's
Most quiet need, by sun and candlelight.
I love thee freely, as men strive for Right;
I love thee purely, as they turn from Praise.
I love thee with the passion put to use
In my old griefs, and with my childhood's faith.
I love thee with a love I seemed to lose
With my lost saints, – I love thee with the breath,
Smiles, tears, of all my life! – and, if God choose,
I shall but love thee better after death.

Meeting at Night

ROBERT BROWNING

(England, 1812-89)

1

The grey sea and the long black land;
And the yellow half-moon large and low;
And the startled little waves that leap
In fiery ringlets from their sleep,
As I gain the cove with pushing prow,
And quench its speed i' the slushy sand.

2

Then a mile of warm sea-scented beach;
Three fields to cross till a farm appears;
A tap at the pane, the quick sharp scratch
And blue spurt of a lighted match,
And a voice less loud, through its joys and fears,
Than the two hearts beating each to each!

Hinterhof

JAMES FENTON

(England, *b.* 1949)

Stay near to me and I'll stay near to you –
As near as you are dear to me will do,
        Near as the rainbow to the rain,
        The west wind to the windowpane,
As fire to the hearth, as dawn to dew.

Stay true to me and I'll stay true to you –
As true as you are new to me will do,
        New as the rainbow in the spray,
        Utterly new in every way,
New in the way that what you say is true.

Stay near to me, stay true to me. I'll stay
As near, as true to you as heart could pray.
        Heart never hoped that one might be
        Half of the things you are to me –
The dawn, the fire, the rainbow and the day.

A Pavane for the Nursery

WILLIAM JAY SMITH
(USA, *b.* 1918)

Now touch the air softly, step gently, one, two...
I'll love you till roses are robin's-egg blue;
I'll love you till gravel is eaten for bread,
And lemons are orange, and lavender's red.

Now touch the air softly, swing gently the broom.
I'll love you till windows are all of a room;
And the table is laid, and the table is bare,
And the ceiling reposes on bottomless air.

I'll love you till heaven rips the stars from his coat,
And the moon rows away in a glass-bottomed boat;
And Orion steps down like a diver below,
And earth is ablaze, and ocean aglow.

So touch the air softly, and swing the broom high.
We will dust the gray mountains, and sweep the blue sky;
And I'll love you as long as the furrow the plow,
As however is ever, and ever is now.

The Passionate Shepherd to His Love

CHRISTOPHER MARLOWE
(England, 1564-93)

Come live with me and be my love,
And we will all the pleasures prove
That valleys, groves, hills and fields,
Woods, or steepy mountain yields.

And we will sit upon the rocks,
Seeing the shepherds feed their flocks,
By shallow rivers to whose falls
Melodious birds sing madrigals.

And I will make thee beds of roses
And a thousand fragrant posies,
A cap of flowers, and a kirtle
Embroidered all with leaves of myrtle;

A gown made of the finest wool
Which from our pretty lambs we pull,
Fair linèd slippers for the cold,
With buckles of the purest gold.

A belt of straw and ivy-buds,
With coral clasps and amber studs,
And if these pleasures may thee move,
Come live with me, and be my love.

The shepherds' swains shall dance and sing
For thy delight each May morning
If these delights thy mind may move,
Then live with me, and be my love.

A Red, Red Rose

ROBERT BURNS

(Scotland, 1759-96)

My luve is like a red, red rose,
   That's newly sprung in June;
My luve is like the melodie,
   That's sweetly played in tune.
As fair art thou, my bonie lass,
   So deep in luve am I,
And I will luve thee still, my dear,
   Till a' the seas gang dry:

Till a' the seas gang dry, my dear,
   And the rocks melt wi' the sun!
And I will luve thee still, my dear,
   While the sands o' life shall run.
And fare-thee-weel, my only luve,
   And fare-thee-weel a while!
And I will come again, my luve,
   Tho' it were ten-thousand mile.

Valentine

CARAL ANN DUFFY
(Scotland, *b.* 1955)

Not a red rose or a satin heart.

I give you an onion.
It is a moon wrapped in brown paper.
It promises light
like the careful undressing of love.

Here.
It will blind you with tears
like a lover.
It will make your reflection
a wobbling photo of grief.

I am trying to be truthful.

Not a cute card or a kissogram.

I give you an onion.
Its fierce kiss will stay on your lips,
possessive and faithful
as we are,
for as long as we are.

Take it.
Its platinum loops shrink to a wedding-ring,
if you like.
Lethal.
Its scent will cling to your fingers,
cling to your knife.

Valentine

JOHN FULLER
(England, *b.* 1937)

The things about you I appreciate
    May seem indelicate:
I'd like to find you in the shower
And chase the soap for half an hour.
I'd like to have you in my power
    And see your eyes dilate.
I'd like to have your back to scour
And other parts to lubricate.
Sometimes I feel it is my fate
To chase you screaming up a tower
    Or make you cower
By asking you to differentiate
    Nietzsche from Schopenhauer.
I'd like successfully to guess your weight
    And win you at a fête.
I'd like to offer you a flower.

I like the hair upon your shoulders,
Falling like water over boulders.
I like the shoulders, too: they are essential.
Your collar-bones have great potential
(I'd like all your particulars in folders
    Marked *Confidential*).

I like your cheeks, I like your nose,
I like the way your lips disclose
The neat arrangement of your teeth
(Half above and half beneath)
    In rows.

I like your eyes, I like their fringes.
The way they focus on me gives me twinges.
Your upper arms drive me berserk.
I like the way your elbows work,
    On hinges.

I like your wrists, I like your glands,
I like the fingers on your hands.
I'd like to teach them how to count,
And certain things we might exchange,
Something familiar for something strange,
I'd like to give you just the right amount
    And get some change.

I like it when you tilt your cheek up.
I like the way you nod and hold a teacup.
I like your legs when you unwind them.
Even in trousers I don't mind them.
I like each softly-moulded kneecap.
I like the little crease behind them.
I'd always know, without a recap,
    Where to find them.

I like the sculpture of your ears.
I like the way your profile disappears
Whenever you decide to turn and face me.
I'd like to cross two hemispheres
    And have you chase me.
I'd like to smuggle you across frontiers
Or sail with you at night into Tangiers.
    I'd like you to embrace me.

I'd like to see you ironing your skirt
        And cancelling other dates,
I'd like to button up your shirt.
I like the way your chest inflates.
I'd like to soothe you when you're hurt
Or frightened senseless by invert-
        ebrates.

I'd like you even if you were malign
And had a yen for sudden homicide.
I'd let you put insecticide
        Into my wine.
I'd even like you if you were the Bride
        Of Frankenstein
Or something ghoulish out of Mamoulian's
        Jekyll and Hyde.
I'd even like you as my Julian
Of Norwich or Cathleen ní Houlihan.
        How melodramatic
If you were something muttering in attics
Like Mrs Rochester or a student of Boolean
        Mathematics.

You are the end of self-abuse.
You are the eternal feminine.
I'd like to find a good excuse
To call on you and find you in.
I'd like to put my hand beneath your chin.
        And see you grin.
I'd like to taste your Charlotte Russe,
I'd like to feel my lips upon your skin,
I'd like to make you reproduce.

I'd like you in my confidence.
I'd like to be your second look.
I'd like to let you try the French Defence
And mate you with my rook.
I'd like to be your preference
And hence
I'd like to be around when you unhook.
I'd like to be your only audience,
The final name in your appointment book,
Your future tense.

Conviction IV

STEVIE SMITH

(England, 1902-71)

I like to get off with people,
I like to lie in their arms
I like to be held and lightly kissed,
Safe from all alarms.

I like to laugh and be happy
With a beautiful kiss,
I tell you, in all the world
There is no bliss like this.

Please Can I Have a Man

SELIMA HILL

(England, *b.* 1945)

Please can I have a man who wears corduroy.
Please can I have a man
who knows the names of 100 different roses;
who doesn't mind my absent-minded rabbits
wandering in and out
as if they own the place,
who makes me creamy curries from fresh lemon-grass,
who walks like Belmondo in *A Bout de Souffle*;
who sticks all my carefully-selected postcards –
sent from exotic cities
he doesn't expect to come with me to,
but would if I asked, which I will do –
with nobody else's, up on his bedroom wall,
starting with Ivy, the Famous Diving Pig,
whose picture, in action, I bought ten copies of;
who talks like Belmondo too, with lips as smooth
and tightly-packed as chocolate-coated
(*melting* chocolate) peony buds;
who knows that piling himself stubbornly on top of me
like a duvet stuffed with library books and shopping-bags
is all too easy: please can I have a man
who is not prepared to do that.
Who is not prepared to say I'm 'pretty' either.
Who, when I come trotting in from the bathroom
like a squealing freshly-scrubbed piglet
that likes nothing better than a binge
of being affectionate and undisciplined and uncomplicated,
opens his arms like a trough for me to dive into.

Lovers' Words

DAVID CAMPBELL

(Australia, 1915-79)

Like swallows, no, like hawks they live
And take the minute on the wing
And pick it bare. Love is a thing
They seek to prove or else disprove.
Selfish, unstable, on the move,
They die unless an eagle sing,
While we have time for hovering,
To brood a season on our love.

O lovers' words are mostly lies,
Their cross-my-heart and I-love-you
Are lessons learned to win a prize,
Extorted, or for payment due.
How sweet it is with open eyes
To say, I love, when it is true.

She Walks in Beauty

LORD BYRON

(England, 1788-1824)

She walks in beauty, like the night
   Of cloudless climes and starry skies;
And all that's best of dark and bright
   Meet in her aspect and her eyes:
Thus mellowed to that tender light
   Which heaven to gaudy day denies.

One shade the more, one ray the less,
   Had half impaired the nameless grace
Which waves in every raven tress,
   Or softly lightens o'er her face;
Where thoughts serenely sweet express
   How pure, how dear their dwelling place.

And on that cheek, and o'er that brow,
   So soft, so calm, yet eloquent,
The smiles that win, the tints that glow,
   But tell of days in goodness spent,
A mind at peace with all below,
   A heart whose love is innocent!

Love's Philosophy

PERCY BYSSHE SHELLEY
(England, 1792-1822)

The fountains mingle with the river,
And the rivers with the ocean,
The winds of heaven mix for ever
With a sweet emotion;
Nothing in the world is single;
All things by a law divine
In one another's being mingle –
Why not I with thine?

See the mountains kiss high heaven,
And the waves clasp one another;
No sister flower would be forgiven
If it disdained its brother:
And the sunlight clasps the earth,
And the moonbeams kiss the sea,
What are all these kissings worth,
If thou kiss not me?

'Time to live and let love, Lesbia...'

CATULLUS

(Imperial Rome, *c.*84–*c.*54 BC)

translated from the Latin
by JOSEPHINE BALMER

Time to live and let love, Lesbia,
count old men's cant, their carping chatter,
cheap talk, not worth one last penny piece.
You see, suns can set, can rise again
but when our brief light begins to wane
night brings on one long unending sleep.
So let me have a thousand kisses,
then a hundred, a thousand *gratis*,
a hundred, a thousand, on increase.
Then, when we've made our first million,
we can cook the books, just smudge the sums
so no evil eye can spy, sully,
by reckoning up our final tally.

To His Coy Mistress

ANDREW MARVELL

(England, 1621-78)

Had we but world enough, and time,
This coyness, Lady, were no crime.
We would sit down, and think which way
To walk, and pass our long love's day.
Thou by the Indian Ganges' side
Shouldst rubies find: I by the tide
Of Humber would complain. I would
Love you ten years before the flood:
And you should, if you please, refuse
Till the conversion of the Jews.
My vegetable love should grow
Vaster than empires, and more slow.
An hundred years should go to praise
Thine eyes, and on thy forehead gaze.
Two hundred to adore each breast:
But thirty thousand to the rest.
An age at least to every part,
And the last age should show your heart:
For, Lady, you deserve this state;
Nor would I love at lower rate.
  But at my back I always hear
Time's wingèd chariot hurrying near:
And yonder all before us lie
Deserts of vast eternity.
Thy beauty shall no more be found;
Nor, in thy marble vault, shall sound
My echoing song: then worms shall try
That long-preserved virginity:
And your quaint honour turn to dust;
And into ashes all my lust.

The grave's a fine and private place,
But none, I think, do there embrace.
   Now, therefore, while the youthful glue
Sits on thy skin like morning dew,
And while thy willing soul transpires
At every pore with instant fires,
Now let us sport us while we may;
And now, like amorous birds of prey,
Rather at once our time devour,
Than languish in his slow-chapped power.
Let us roll all our strength, and all
Our sweetness, up into one ball:
And tear our pleasures with rough strife,
Thorough the iron grates of life.
Thus, though we cannot make our sun
Stand still, yet we will make him run.

In Defence of Adultery

JULIA COPUS
(England, *b.* 1969)

We don't fall in love: it rises through us
the way that certain music does –
whether a symphony or ballad –
and it is sepia-coloured,
like tea that stains as it creeps up
the tiny tube-like gaps inside
a cube of sugar lying by a cup.
Yes, love's like that: just when we least
needed or expected it
a part of us dips into it
by chance or mishap and it seeps
through our capillaries, it clings
inside the chambers of the heart
to atriums and ventricles. We're
victims, we say: merely vessels
drinking the vanilla scent
of this one's skin, the lustre
of another's blue eyes skilfully
darkened with bistre. And whatever
damage might result we're not
to blame for it: love is an autocrat
and won't be disobeyed.
Sometimes we almost manage
to convince ourselves of that.

Upon Julia's Clothes

ROBERT HERRICK

(England, 1591-1674)

When as in silks my Julia goes,
Then, then (methinks) how sweetly flows
That liquefaction of her clothes.

Next, when I cast mine eyes and see
That brave vibration each way free;
O how that glittering taketh me!

A Birthday

CHRISTINA ROSSETTI

(England, 1830-94)

My heart is like a singing bird
   Whose nest is in a watered shoot;
My heart is like an apple tree
   Whose boughs are bent with thickset fruit;
My heart is like a rainbow shell
   That paddles in a halcyon sea;
My heart is gladder than all these
   Because my love is come to me.

Raise me a daïs of silk and down;
   Hang it with vair and purple dyes;
Carve it in doves and pomegranates,
   And peacocks with a hundred eyes;
Work it in gold and silver grapes,
   In leaves and silver fleurs-de-lys;
Because the birthday of my life
   Is come, my love is come to me.

The Good Morrow

JOHN DONNE

(England, 1572-1631)

I wonder by my troth, what thou, and I
  Did, till we loved? were we not weaned till then,
But sucked on country pleasures, childishly?
  Or snorted we in the seven sleepers' den?
'Twas so; but this, all pleasures fancies be.
If ever any beauty I did see,
Which I desired, and got, 'twas but a dream of thee.

And now good morrow to our waking souls,
  Which watch not one another out of fear;
For love, all love of other sights controls,
  And makes one little room, an every where.
Let sea-discoverers to new worlds have gone,
Let maps to others, worlds on worlds have shown,
Let us possess one world, each hath one, and is one.

My face in thine eye, thine in mine appears,
  And true plain hearts do in the faces rest,
Where can we find two better hemispheres
  Without sharp north, without declining west?
What ever dies, was not mixed equally;
If our two loves be one, or, thou and I
Love so alike, that none do slacken, none can die.

FROM

Trilogy for X

LOUIS MACNEICE

(Ireland, 1907-63)

And love hung still as crystal over the bed
   And filled the corners of the enormous room;
The boom of dawn that left her sleeping, showing
   The flowers mirrored in the mahogany table.

O my love, if only I were able
   To protract this hour of quiet after passion,
Not ration happiness but keep this door for ever
   Closed on the world, its own world closed within it.

But dawn's waves trouble with the bubbling minute,
   The names of books come clear upon their shelves,
The reason delves for duty and you will wake
   With a start and go on living on your own.

The first train passes and the windows groan,
   Voices will hector and your voice become
A drum in tune with theirs, which all last night
   Like sap that fingered through a hungry tree
Asserted our one night's identity.

Song for a Lady

ANNE SEXTON
(USA, 1928-74)

On the day of breasts and small hips
the window pocked with bad rain,
rain coming on like a minister,
we coupled, so sane and insane.
We lay like spoons while the sinister
rain dropped like flies on our lips
and our glad eyes and our small hips.

'The room is so cold with rain,' you said
and you, feminine you, with your flower
said novenas to my ankles and elbows.
You are a national product and power.
Oh my swan, my drudge, my dear wooly rose,
even a notary would notarise our bed
as you knead me and I rise like bread.

On a Night of the Full Moon

AUDRE LORDE
(USA, 1934-92)

I

Out of my flesh that hungers
and my mouth that knows
comes the shape I am seeking
for reason.
The curve of your waiting body
fits my waiting hand
your breasts warm as sunlight
your lips quick as young birds
between your thighs the sweet
sharp taste of limes.

Thus I hold you
frank in my heart's eye
in my skin's knowing
as my fingers conceive your warmth
I feel your stomach
move against mine.

Before the moon wanes again
we shall come together.

II

And I would be the moon
spoken over your beckoning flesh
breaking against reservations
beaching thought
my hands at your high tide

over and under inside you
and the passing of hungers
attended   forgotten.

Darkly risen
the moon speaks
my eyes
judging   your roundness
delightful.

'As our bloods separate'

DAVID CONSTANTINE

(England, *b.* 1944)

As our bloods separate the clock resumes,
I hear the wind again as our hearts quieten.
We were a ring: the clock ticked round us
For that time and the wind was deflected.

The clock pecks everything to the bone.
The wind enters through the broken eyes
Of houses and through their wide mouths
And scatters the ashes from the hearth.

Sleep. Do not let go my hand.

New Year's Eve

D. H. LAWRENCE

(England, 1885-1930)

There are only two things now,
The great black night scooped out
And this fireglow.

This fireglow, the core,
And we the two ripe pips
That are held in store.

Listen, the darkness rings
As it circulates round our fire.
Take off your things.

Your shoulders, your bruised throat!
Your breasts, your nakedness!
This fiery coat!

As the darkness flickers and dips,
As the firelight falls and leaps
From your feet to your lips!

Last Night

SHARON OLDS
(USA, *b.* 1942)

The next day, I am almost afraid.
Love? It was more like dragonflies
in the sun, 100 degrees at noon,
the ends of their abdomens stuck together, I
close my eyes when I remember. I hardly
knew myself, like something twisting and
twisting out of a chrysalis,
enormous, without language, all
head, all shut eyes, and the humming
like madness, the way they writhe away,
and do not leave, back, back,
away, back. Did I know you? No kiss,
no tenderness – more like killing, death-grip
holding to life, genitals
like violent hands clasped tight
barely moving, more like being closed
in a great jaw and eaten, and the screaming
I groan to remember it, and when we started
to die, then I refuse to remember,
the way a drunkard forgets. After,
you held my hands extremely hard as my
body moved in shudders like the ferry when its
axle is loosed past engagement, you kept me
sealed exactly against you, our hairlines
wet as the arc of a gateway after
a cloudburst, you secured me in your arms till I slept –
that was love, and we woke in the morning
clasped, fragrant, buoyant, that was
the morning after love.

'Shall I compare thee to a summer's day?'

WILLIAM SHAKESPEARE

(England, 1564-1616)

Shall I compare thee to a summer's day?
Thou art more lovely and more temperate.
Rough winds do shake the darling buds of May,
And summer's lease hath all too short a date.
Sometime too hot the eye of heaven shines,
And often is his gold complexion dimmed;
And every fair from fair sometime declines,
By chance or nature's changing course untrimmed.
But thy eternal summer shall not fade,
Nor lose possession of that fair thou ow'st,
Nor shall Death brag thou wand'rest in his shade,
When in eternal lines to time thou grow'st.
So long as men can breathe or eyes can see,
So long lives this, and this gives life to thee.

'My mistress' eyes are nothing like the sun'

WILLIAM SHAKESPEARE

(England, 1564-1616)

My mistress' eyes are nothing like the sun;
Coral is far more red than her lip's red;
If snow be white, why then her breasts are dun;
If hairs be wires, black wires grow on her head.
I have seen roses damasked, red and white,
But no such roses see I in her cheeks,
And in some perfumes is there more delight
Than in the breath that from my mistress reeks.
I love to hear her speak, yet well I know
That music hath a far more pleasing sound.
I grant I never saw a goddess go;
My mistress when she walks treads on the ground.
And yet, by heaven, I think my love as rare
As any she belied with false compare.

Late Love

JACKIE KAY
(Scotland, *b.* 1961)

How they strut about, people in love,
how tall they grow, pleased with themselves,
their hair, glossy, their skin shining.
They don't remember who they have been.

How filmic they are just for this time.
How important they've become – secret, above
the order of things, the dreary mundane.
Every church bell ringing, a fresh sign.

How dull the lot that are not in love.
Their clothes shabby, their skin lustreless;
how clueless they are, hair a mess; how they trudge
up and down streets in the rain,

remembering one kiss in a dark alley,
a touch in a changing-room, if lucky, a lovely wait
for the phone to ring, maybe, baby.
The past with its rush of velvet, its secret hush

already miles away, dimming now, in the late day.

Last Love

FYODOR TYUTCHEV

(Russia, 1803-73)

translated from the Russian
by VLADIMIR NABOKOV

Love at the closing of our days
is apprehensive and very tender.
Glow brighter, brighter, farewell rays
of one last love in its evening splendour.

Blue shade takes half the world away:
through western clouds alone some light is slanted.
O tarry, O tarry, declining day,
enchantment, let me stay enchanted.

The blood runs thinner, yet the heart
remains as ever deep and tender.
O last belated love, thou art
a blend of joy and of hopeless surrender.

'Bright star…'

JOHN KEATS

(England, 1795-1821)

Bright star, would I were stedfast as thou art –
  Not in lone splendour hung aloft the night,
And watching, with eternal lids apart.
  Like nature's patient, sleepless Eremite.
The moving waters at their priestlike task
  Of pure ablution round earth's human shores,
Or gazing on the new soft-fallen mask
  Of snow upon the mountains and the moors –
No – yet still stedfast, still unchangeable.
  Pillow'd upon my fair love's ripening breast,
To feel for ever its soft swell and fall,
  Awake for ever in a sweet unrest,
Still, still to hear her tender-taken breath,
And so live ever – or else swoon to death.

3.

DESSERT

Passionfood's dessert is a selection of deliciously saucy or tender poems by leading modern poets. It also features one very contemporary contribution (70) by the Roman satirist Petronius, author of the *Satyricon* (turned into a film by Fellini), of whom Tacitus wrote: 'His days he passed in sleep, his nights in the business and pleasures of life. The reputation that most men win by energy he achieved by idleness.'

Best-known for his fiction, Canadian writer Michael Ondaatje was born in Ceylon (now Sri Lanka), growing up in an extraordinary home portrayed in his semi-autobiographical memoir *Running in the Family*. That exotic background also informs many of the poems in his book *The Cinnamon Peeler*, notably the title-poem itself (80).

A reformed alcoholic, Raymond Carver found happiness with fellow writer Tess Gallagher for the last eleven years of his life, a time evoked in their two poems here (74 & 75), which was also when most of Carver's short stories and poetry were published to wide acclaim.

Ecstasy

SHARON OLDS
(USA, *b.* 1942)

As we made love for the third day,
cloudy and dark, as we did not stop
but went into it and into it and
did not hesitate and did not hold back we
rose through the air, until we were up above
timber line. The lake lay
icy and silver, the surface shirred,
reflecting nothing. The black rocks
lifted around it into the grainy
sepia air, the patches of snow
brilliant white, and even though we
did not know where we were, we could not
speak the language, we could hardly see, we
did not stop, rising with the black
rocks to the black hills, the black
mountains rising from the hills. Resting
on the crest of the mountains, one huge
cloud with scalloped edges of blazing
evening light, we did not turn back,
we stayed with it, even though we were
far beyond what we knew, we rose
into the grain of the cloud, even though we were
frightened, the air hollow, even though
nothing grew there, even though it is a
place from which no one has ever come back.

Pentecost

MICHAEL DONAGHY
(USA / England,
1954-2004)

The neighbours hammered on the walls all night,
Outraged by the noise we made in bed.
Still we kept it up until by first light
We'd said everything that could be said.

Undaunted, we began to mewl and roar
As if desire had stripped itself of words.
Remember when we made those sounds before?
When we built a tower heavenwards
They were our reward for blasphemy.
And then again, two thousand years ago,
We huddled in a room in Galilee
Speaking languages we didn't know,
While amethyst uraeuses of flame
Hissed above us. We recalled the tower
And the tongues. We knew this was the same,
But love had turned the curse into a power.

See? It's something that we've always known:
Though we command the language of desire,
The voice of ecstasy is not our own.
We long to lose ourselves amid the choir
Of the salmon twilight and the mackerel sky,
The very air we take into our lungs,
And the rhododendron's cry.

And when you lick the sweat along my thigh,
Dearest, we renew the gift of tongues.

Muse

JO SHAPCOTT
(England, *b.* 1953)

When I kiss you in all the folding places
of your body, you make that noise like a dog
dreaming, dreaming of the long runs he makes
in answer to some jolt to his hormones,
running across landfills, running, running
by tips and shorelines from the scent of too much,
but still going with head up and snout
in the air because he loves it all
and has to get away. I have to kiss deeper
and more slowly – your neck, your inner arm,
the neat creases under your toes, the shadow
behind your knee, the white angles of your groin –
until you fall quiet because only then
can I get the damned words to come into my mouth.

We Did It

YEHUDA AMICHAI
(Germany / Israel,
1924-2000)

translated from the Hebrew
by HAROLD SCHIMMEL

We did it in front of the mirror
And in the light. We did it in darkness,
In water, and in the high grass.

We did it in honour of man
And in honour of beast and in honour of God.
But they didn't want to know about us,
They'd already seen our sort.

We did it with imagination and colours,
With confusion of reddish hair and brown
And with difficult gladdening
Exercises. We did it
Like wheels and holy creatures
And with chariot-feats of prophets.
We did it six wings
And six legs
                                        But the heavens
Were hard above us
Like the earth of the summer beneath.

Doing

PETRONIUS

(Rome, 1st century AD)

translated from the Latin by BEN JONSON (1572-1637)

Doing, a filthy pleasure is, and short;
And done, we straight repent us of the sport:
Let us not then rush blindly on unto it,
Like lustful beasts, that only know to do it:
For lust will languish, and that heat decay.
But thus, thus, keeping endless holiday,
Let us together closely lie and kiss,
There is no labour, nor no shame in this;
This hath pleased, doth please, and long will please; never
Can this decay, but is beginning ever.

'may I feel said he...'

E. E. CUMMINGS

(USA, 1894-1962)

may i feel said he
(I'll squeal said she
just once said he)
it's fun said she

(may i touch said he
how much said she
a lot said he)
why not said she

(let's go said he
not too far said she
what's too far said he
where you are said she)

may i stay said he
(which way said she
like this said he
if you kiss said she

may i move said he
is it love said she)
if you're willing said he
(but you're killing said she

but it's life said he
but your wife said she
now said he)
ow said she

(tiptop said he
don't stop said she
oh no said he)
go slow said she

(cccome?said he
ummm said she)
you're divine!said he
(you are Mine said she)

That Day

NIKKI GIOVANNI
(USA, *b.* 1943)

if you've got the key
then i've got the door
let's do what we did
when we did it before

if you've got the time
i've got the way
let's do what we did
when we did it all day

you get the glass
i've got the wine
we'll do what we did
when we did it overtime

if you've got the dough
then i've got the heat
we can use my oven
till it's warm and sweet

i know i'm bold
coming on like this
but the good things in life
are too good to be missed

now time is money
and money is sweet
if you're busy baby
we can do it on our feet

we can do it on the floor
we can do it on the stair
we can do it on the couch
we can do it in the air

we can do it in the grass
and in case we get an itch
i can scratch it with my left hand
'cause i'm really quite a witch

if we do it once a month
we can do it in time
if we do it once a week
we can do it in rhyme
if we do it every day
we can do it everyway
we can do it like we did it
when we did it
that day

Looking at Each Other

MURIEL RUKEYSER
(USA, 1913-80)

Yes, we were looking at each other
Yes, we knew each other very well
Yes, we had made love with each other many times
Yes, we had heard music together
Yes, we had gone to the sea together
Yes, we had cooked and eaten together
Yes, we had laughed often day and night
Yes, we fought violence and knew violence
Yes, we hated the inner and outer oppression
Yes, that day we were looking at each other
Yes, we saw the sunlight pouring down
Yes, the corner of the table was between us
Yes, bread and flowers were on the table
Yes, our eyes saw each other's eyes
Yes, our mouths saw each other's mouth
Yes, our breasts saw each other's breasts
Yes, our bodies entire saw each other
Yes, it was beginning in each
Yes, it threw waves across our lives
Yes, the pulses were becoming very strong
Yes, the beating became very delicate
Yes, the calling   the arousal
Yes, the arriving   the coming
Yes, there it was for both entire
Yes, we were looking at each other

'Keep your eyes open when you kiss...'

JOHN BERRYMAN

(USA, 1914-72)

Keep your eyes open when you kiss: do: when
You kiss. All silly time else, close them to;
Unsleeping, I implore you (dear) pursue
In darkness me, as I do you again
Instantly we part . . only me both then
And when your fingers fall, let there be two
Only, 'in that dream kingdom': I would have you
Me alone recognise your citizen.

Before who wanted eyes, making love, so?
I do now. However we are driven and hide,
What state we keep all other states condemn,
We see ourselves, we watch the solemn glow
Of empty courts we kiss in . . Open wide!
You do, you do, and I look into them.

Behind Which There Is an Expanse Past the World

TESS GALLAGHER
(USA, *b.* 1943)

When it's time to come into her
she says he always turns the light on
because he likes to look at her. Not at, but into.
At the eyes. As if the receiving he wanted
needed to reach beyond the geometry of pursuit, to use
the mind's fixative to close it in, or to be
sure of its sending. But also, she said, she felt it
was his way of actually going further into space
at all points of the body. Because he knew, of course,
that other men didn't have to be most bright so soon.
His gaze was steeple-shaped,

like an embodied triangle, moving out from the eyes
to where he joined her as apex, and into which
both lovers, and lovers before them, had
possibly disappeared, never to be retrieved. Except
once in a while as a child, or as the wish
for a child, the lovemaking carried past volition
into an extension of the triangle's
inner space. And future times into which
the lovers do, in fact, disappear, and leave the triangle
altogether behind, as in that moment when space
reviews its options and means what it's brought
together, the way a rainbow wants to pass

attention on to the imagined, yet unattainable,
treasure, even as its color is avoidance of attention
elsewhere. If the man were making love to
a rainbow he would have to look at it, and
yes, he might. But I am looking with

her man into myself as that lover. That's
the way the triangle is. Suddenly
you're inside. And so is
the world.

The Best Time of the Day

RAYMOND CARVER

(USA, 1939-88)

Cool summer nights.
Windows open.
Lamps burning.
Fruit in the bowl.
And your head on my shoulder.
These the happiest moments in the day.

Next to the early morning hours,
of course. And the time
just before lunch.
And the afternoon, and
early evening hours.
But I do love

these summer nights.
Even more, I think,
than those other times.
The work finished for the day.
And no one who can reach us now.
Or ever.

Invitation

GRACE NICHOLS
(Guyana / England,
b. 1950)

1

If my fat
was too much for me
I would have told you
I would have lost a stone
or two

I would have gone jogging
even when it was fogging
I would have weighed in
sitting the bathroom scale
with my tail tucked in

I would have dieted
more care a diabetic

But as it is
I'm feeling fine
feel no need
to change my lines
when I move I'm target light

Come up and see me sometime

2

Come up and see me sometime
Come up and see me sometime

My breasts are huge exciting
amnions of water melon
                        your hands can't cup
my thighs are twin seals
                        fat as slick pups
there's a purple cherry
below the blues
                        of my black seabelly
there's a mole that gets a ride
each time I shift the heritage
of my behind

Come up and see me sometime

The Cinnamon Peeler

MICHAEL ONDAATJE

(Sri Lanka / Canada,
b. 1943)

If I were a cinnamon peeler
I would ride your bed
and leave the yellow bark dust
on your pillow.

Your breast and shoulders would reek
you could never walk through markets
without the profession of my fingers
floating over you. The blind would
stumble certain of whom they approached
though you might bathe
under rain gutters, monsoon.

Here on the upper thigh
at this smooth pasture
neighbour to your hair
or the crease
that cuts your back. This ankle.
You will be known among strangers
as the cinnamon peeler's wife.

I could hardly glance at you
before marriage
never touch you
– your keen-nosed mother, your rough brothers.
I buried my hands
in saffron, disguised them
over smoking tar,
helped the honey gatherers...

When we swam once
I touched you in water
and our bodies remained free,
you could hold me and be blind of smell.
You climbed the bank and said

                    this is how you touch other women
the grass cutter's wife, the lime burner's daughter.
And you searched your arms
for the missing perfume

                                        and knew

                        what good is it
to be the lime burner's daughter
left with no trace
as if not spoken to in the act of love
as if wounded without the pleasure of a scar.

You touched
your belly to my hands
in the dry air and said
I am the cinnamon
peeler's wife. Smell me.

Raisin pumpernickel

MARGE PIERCY
(USA, *b.* 1936)

You shine, my love, like a sugar maple in October,
a golden-orange overarching blaze of leaves,
each painted its own tint of flames
tossed on the ground bright as silk scarves.
So are you happy.

My curly one, my stubborn fierce butter,
down with the head and charge all horns
and the blattering thunk of bone head on bone,
the smoke and hot rubber stench of overheated temper.
So are you angry.

The tomcat is a ready lover. He can do it at dawn
when the birds are still yawning, he can do it
while the houseguest walks up the drive, do it after
four parties and an all-night dance, on a convenient floor.
So are you able.

Your love comes down rich as the warm spring rain.
Now it charges like a tawny dark maned lion.
Now it envelopes me in wraiths of silken mist.
Now it is a thick hot soup that sustains me.
So are you loving.

You're an endless sink of love, a gaping maw
into which I shovel attention like soft coal
into an old furnace; you're a limitless love source,
a great underground spring surging out of rock
to feed a river.

You cry your needs, bold as a six-week kitten.
You're devious as a corporate takeover and direct
as an avalanche. What ten years into this conversation
commands my interest? You're still the best novel
I've ever read.

Secretly we both think we were bred for each other
as part of an experiment in getting dreams made
flesh and then having to feed on the daily bread
of passion. So we die and die with loving
and go on living.

My Belovèd Compares Herself to a Pint of Stout

PAUL DURCAN

(Ireland, *b.* 1944)

When in the heat of the first night of summer
I observe with a whistle of envy
That Jackson has driven out the road for a pint of stout,
She puts her arm around my waist and scolds me:
Am I not your pint of stout? Drink me.
There is nothing except, of course, self-pity
To stop you also having your pint of stout.

Putting self-pity on a leash in the back of the car,
I drive out the road, do a U-turn,
Drive in the hall door, up the spiral staircase,
Into her bedroom. I park at the foot of her bed,
Nonchalantly step out leaving the car unlocked,
Stroll over to the chest of drawers, lean on it,
Circumspectly inspect the backs of my hands,
Modestly request from her a pint of stout.
She turns her back, undresses, pours herself into bed,
Adjusts the pillows, slaps her hand on the coverlet:
Here I am – at the very least
Look at my new cotton nightdress before you shred it
And do not complain that I have not got a head on me.

I look around to see her foaming out of the bedclothes
Not laughing but gazing at me out of four-leggèd eyes.
She says: Close your eyes, put your hands around me.
I am the blackest, coldest pint you will ever drink
So sip me slowly, let me linger on your lips,
Ooze through your teeth, dawdle down your throat,
Before swooping down into your guts.

While you drink me I will deposit my scum
On your rim and when you get to the bottom of me,
No matter how hard you try to drink my dregs –
And being a man, you will, no harm in that –
I will keep bubbling up back at you.
For there is no escaping my aftermath.
Tonight – being the first night of summer –
You may drink as many pints of me as you like.
There are barrels of me in the tap room.
In thin daylight at nightfall,
You will fall asleep drunk on love.
When you wake early in the early morning
You will have a hangover,
All chaste, astringent, aflame with affirmation,
Straining at the bit to get to first mass
And holy communion and work – the good life.

'i like my body when it is with your...'

E. E. CUMMINGS
(USA, 1894-1962)

i like my body when it is with your
body. It is so quite new a thing.
Muscles better and nerves more.
i like your body. i like what it does,
i like its hows. i like to feel the spine
of your body and its bones, and the trembling
-firm-smooth ness and which i will
again and again and again
kiss, i like kissing this and that of you,
i like,slowly stroking the,shocking fuzz
of your electric fur,and what-is-it comes
over parting flesh....And eyes big love-crumbs,

and possibly i like the thrill

of under me you so quite new

4.

FRUIT

These poems bear the fruit of passion: deeper love, the kind of love that lasts. They show many ways in which love can grow through friendship to fill every part of our lives. Many are celebrations of closeness, trust and mutual understanding, poems of joy, wisdom and shared recognition.

The poem by Sir Philip Sidney (107) exists in two versions. Originally a famous sonnet spoken by a shepherdess (hence the gender) in a romance known as *The Old Arcadia*, it was printed after Sidney's death in an altered form as a ten-line song. The latter version, more effective as a separate poem, is the one I've chosen to include.

'The minute I heard my first love story...'

RUMI
(Persia, 1207-73)

translated from the Persian
by COLEMAN BARKS
with JOHN MOYNE

The minute I heard my first love story
I started looking for you, not knowing
how blind that was.

Lovers don't finally meet somewhere.
They're in each other all along.

The Confirmation

EDWIN MUIR

(Scotland, 1887-1959)

Yes, yours, my love, is the right human face.
I in my mind had waited for this long,
Seeing the false and searching for the true,
Then found you as a traveller finds a place
Of welcome suddenly amid the wrong
Valleys and rocks and twisting roads. But you,
What shall I call you? A fountain in a waste,
A well of water in a country dry,
Or anything that's honest and good, an eye
That makes the whole world bright. Your open heart,
Simple with giving, gives the primal deed,
The first good world, the blossom, the blowing seed,
The hearth, the steadfast land, the wandering sea,
Not beautiful or rare in every part.
But like yourself, as they were meant to be.

'Love is not just a function of the eyes...'

MARCUS ARGENTARIUS

(Greece, 20 BC–30 AD)

translated from the Greek
by FLEUR ADCOCK

Love is not just a function of the eyes.
Beautiful objects will, of course, inspire
Possessive urges – you need not despise
Your taste. But when insatiable desire
Inflames you for a girl who's out of fashion,
Lacking in glamour – plain, in fact – that fire
Is genuine; that's the authentic passion.
Beauty, though, any critic can admire.

'There is a garden in her face...'

THOMAS CAMPION

(England, 1567-1620)

There is a garden in her face,
Where roses and white lilies grow;
A heav'nly paradise is that place,
Wherein all pleasant fruits do flow.
    There cherries grow, which none may buy,
    Till 'Cherry ripe' themselves do cry.

Those cherries fairly do enclose
Of orient pearl a double row,
Which when her lovely laughter shows,
They look like rose-buds fill'd with snow.
    Yet them nor peer nor prince can buy,
    Till 'Cherry ripe' themselves do cry.

Her eyes like angels watch them still,
Her brows like bended bows do stand,
Threat'ning with piercing frowns to kill
All that attempt with eye or hand
    Those sacred cherries to come nigh,
    Till 'Cherry ripe' themselves do cry.

Upon the Nipples of Julia's Breast

ROBERT HERRICK

(England, 1591-1674)

Have ye beheld (with much delight)
A red rose peeping through a white?
Or else a cherry (double graced)
Within a lily? Centre placed?
Or ever marked the pretty beam,
A strawberry shows half drowned in cream?
Or seen rich rubies blushing through
A pure smooth pearl, and orient too?
So like to this, nay all the rest,
Is each neat niplet of her breast.

Wild strawberries

HELEN DUNMORE

(England, *b.* 1952)

What I get I bring home to you:
a dark handful, sweet-edged,
dissolving in one mouthful.

I bother to bring them for you
though they're so quickly over,
pulpless, sliding to juice,

a grainy rub on the tongue
and the taste's gone. If you remember
we were in the woods at wild strawberry time

and I was making a basket of dockleaves
to hold what you'd picked,
but the cold leaves unplaited themselves

and slid apart, and again unplaited themselves
until I gave up and ate wild strawberries
out of your hands for sweetness.

I lipped at your palm –
the little salt edge there,
the tang of money you'd handled.

As we stayed in the wood, hidden,
we heard the sound system below us
calling the winners at Chepstow,
faint as the breeze turned.

The sun came out on us, the shade blotches
went hazel: we heard names
bubble like stock-doves over the woods

as jockeys in stained silks gentled
those sweat-dark, shuddering horses
down to the walk.

The Skunk

SEAMUS HEANEY

(Ireland, *b.* 1939)

Up, black, striped and damasked like the chasuble
At a funeral Mass, the skunk's tail
Paraded the skunk. Night after night
I expected her like a visitor.

The refrigerator whinnied into silence.
My desk light softened beyond the verandah.
Small oranges loomed in the orange tree.
I began to be tense as a voyeur.

After eleven years I was composing
Love-letters again, broaching the word 'wife'
Like a stored cask, as if its slender vowel
Had mutated into the night earth and air

Of California. The beautiful, useless
Tang of eucalyptus spelt your absence.
The aftermath of a mouthful of wine
Was like inhaling you off a cold pillow.

And there she was, the intent and glamorous,
Ordinary, mysterious skunk,
Mythologised, demythologised,
Snuffing the boards five feet beyond me.

It all came back to me last night, stirred
By the sootfall of your things at bedtime,
Your head-down, tail-up hunt in a bottom drawer
For the black plunge-line nightdress.

To My Dear and Loving Husband

ANNE BRADSTREET

(England / America, 1612-72)

If ever two were one, then surely we.
If ever man were loved by wife, then thee;
If ever wife was happy in a man,
Compare with me, ye women, if you can.
I prize thy love more than whole mines of gold,
Or all the riches that the East doth hold.
My love is such that rivers cannot quench,
Nor ought but love from thee, give recompence.
Thy love is such I can no way repay,
The heavens reward thee manifold, I pray.
Then while we live, in love let's so persever,
Then when we live no more, we may live ever.

The Shampoo

ELIZABETH BISHOP
(USA, 1911-79)

The still explosions on the rocks,
the lichens, grow
by spreading, gray, concentric shocks.
They have arranged
to meet the rings around the moon, although
within our memories they have not changed.

And since the heavens will attend
as long on us,
you've been, dear friend,
precipitate and pragmatical;
and look what happens. For Time is
nothing if not amenable.

The shooting stars in your black hair
in bright formation
are flocking where,
so straight, so soon?
– Come, let me wash it in this big tin basin,
battered and shiny like the moon.

One Thing at Least

JAMES McAULEY

(Australia, 1917-76)

One thing at least I understood
Practically from the start,
That loving must be learnt by heart
If it's to be any good.

It isn't in the flash of thunder,
But in the silent power to give –
A habit into which we live
Ourselves, and grow to be a wonder.

Some like me are slow to learn:
What's plain can be mysterious still.
Feelings alter, fade, return,

But love stands constant in the will:
It's not alone the touching, seeing,
It's how to mean the other's being.

Friendship

ELIZABETH JENNINGS
(England, 1926-2001)

Such love I cannot analyse;
It does not rest in lips or eyes,
Neither in kisses nor caress.
Partly, I know, it's gentleness

And understanding in one word
Or in brief letters. It's preserved
By trust and by respect and awe.
These are the words I'm feeling for.

Two people, yes, two lasting friends.
The giving comes, the taking ends.
There is no measure for such things.
For this all Nature slows and sings.

Love and Friendship

EMILY BRONTË

(England, 1818-48)

Love is like the wild rose-briar,
Friendship like the holly-tree –
The holly is dark when the rose-briar blooms
But which will bloom most constantly?

The wild-rose briar is sweet in the spring,
Its summer blossoms scent the air;
Yet wait till winter comes again
And who will call the wild-briar fair?

Then scorn the silly rose-wreath now
And deck thee with the holly's sheen,
That when December blights thy brow
He still may leave thy garland green.

Atlas

U.A. FANTHORPE

(England, *b.* 1929)

There is a kind of love called maintenance,
Which stores the WD40 and knows when to use it;

Which checks the insurance, and doesn't forget
The milkman; which remembers to plant bulbs;

Which answers letters; which knows the way
The money goes; which deals with dentists

And Road Fund Tax and meeting trains,
And postcards to the lonely; which upholds

The permanently ricketty elaborate
Structures of living; which is Atlas.

And maintenance is the sensible side of love,
Which knows what time and weather are doing
To my brickwork; insulates my faulty wiring;
Laughs at my dryrotten jokes; remembers
My need for gloss and grouting; which keeps
My suspect edifice upright in air,
As Atlas did the sky.

'If love is chaste...'

MICHELANGELO

(Italy, 1475-1564)

translated from the Italian
by ELIZABETH JENNINGS

If love is chaste, if pity comes from heaven,
If fortune, good or ill, is shared between
Two equal loves, and if one wish can govern
Two hearts, and nothing evil intervene:

If one soul joins two bodies fast for ever
And if, on the same wings, these two can fly,
And if one dart of love can pierce and sever
The vital organs of both equally:

If both love one another with the same
Passion, and if each other's good is sought
By both, if taste and pleasure and desire

Bind such a faithful love-knot, who can claim
Either with envy, scorn, contempt or ire,
The power to untie so fast a knot?

'If thou must love me'

ELIZABETH BARRETT BROWNING

(England, 1806-61)

If thou must love me, let it be for nought
Except for love's sake only. Do not say
'I love her for her smile.. her look.. her way
Of speaking gently,.. for a trick of thought
That falls in well with mine, and certes brought
A sense of pleasant ease on such a day' –
For these things in themselves, Belovèd, may
Be changed or change for thee, – and love, so wrought,
May be unwrought so. Neither love me for
Thine own dear pity's wiping my cheeks dry,
Since one might well forget to weep who bore
Thy comfort long, and lose thy love thereby.
But love me for love's sake, that evermore
Thou mayst love on, through love's eternity.

Ballad of a Shadow

ALICE OSWALD

(England, *b.* 1966)

Take from me my voice and I shall voiceless go
to find you; take from me my face,
I'll treck the hills invisibly,
my strength, and I shall run but keep no pace.

Even in cities, take the sense with which I reason
and I shall seek, but close it in your heart,
keep this and forget this
and this, when we're apart,

will be the shadow game of love.
And I shall love in secret
and I shall love in crowds
and love in darkness, in the quiet

outlet of shadows, and in cities
as a ghost walking unnoticed,
and love with books, using their pages like a wind,
not reading, and with people, latticed

by words but through the lattice loving.
And when at last my love is understood,
with you I shall not love but breathe
and turn by breathing into flesh and blood.

FROM

100 Love Sonnets

PABLO NERUDA

(Chile, 1904-73)

translated from the Spanish by STEPHEN MITCHELL

I don't love you as if you were the salt-rose, topaz
or arrow of carnations that propagate fire:
I love you as certain dark things are loved,
secretly, between the shadow and the soul.

I love you as the plant that doesn't bloom and carries
hidden within itself the light of those flowers,
and thanks to your love, darkly in my body
lives the dense fragrance that rises from the earth.

I love you without knowing how, or when, or from where,
I love you simply, without problems or pride:
I love you in this way because I don't know any other way of loving

but this, in which there is no I or you,
so intimate that your hand upon my chest is my hand,
so intimate that when I fall asleep it is your eyes that close.

The Hug

THOM GUNN
(England / USA,
1929-2004)

It was your birthday, we had drunk and dined
Half of the night with our old friend
Who'd showed us in the end
To a bed I reached in one drunk stride.
Already I lay snug,
And drowsy with the wine dozed on one side.

I dozed, I slept. My sleep broke on a hug,
Suddenly, from behind,
In which the full lengths of our bodies pressed:
Your instep to my heel,
My shoulder-blades against your chest.
It was not sex, but I could feel
The whole strength of your body set,
Or braced, to mine,
And locking me to you
As if we were still twenty-two
When our grand passion had not yet
Become familial.
My quick sleep had deleted all
Of intervening time and place.
I only knew
The stay of your secure firm dry embrace.

This Hour

SHARON OLDS
(USA, *b.* 1942)

We could never really say what it is like,
this hour of drinking wine together
on a hot summer night, in the living-room
with the windows open, in our underwear,
my pants with pale-gold gibbon monkeys on them
gleaming in the heat. We talk about our son
disappearing between the pine boughs,
we could not tell what was chrysalis or
bough and what was him. The wine
is powerful, each mouthful holds
for a moment its amber agate shape,
I think of the sweat I sipped from my father's
forehead the hour before his death. We talk about
those last days – that I was waiting for him to die.
You are lying on the couch, your underpants
a luminous white, your hand resting
relaxed, alongside your penis,
we talk about your father's illness,
your nipple like a pure circle of
something risen to the surface of your chest.
Even if we wanted to,
we could not describe it,
the end of the second glass when I sometimes
weep and you start to get sleepy – I love
to drink and cry with you, and end up
sobbing to a sleeping man, your
long body filling the couch and
draped slightly over the ends, the
untrained soft singing of your snore, it cannot be given.

Yes, we know we will make love, but we're
not getting ready to make love,
nor are we getting over making love,
love is simply our element,
it is the summer night, we are in it.

'My true love hath my heart...'

SIR PHILIP SIDNEY

(England, 1554-86)

My true love hath my heart and I have his,
By just exchange one for another given:
I hold his dear, and mine he cannot miss,
There never was a better bargain driven.
My true-love hath my heart and I have his.

His heart in me keeps him and me in one,
My heart in him his thoughts and senses guides.
He loves my heart, for once it was his own:
I cherish his, because in me it bides:
My true love hath my heart, and I have his.

True Love

SHARON OLDS
(USA, *b.* 1942)

In the middle of the night, when we get up
after making love, we look at each other in
complete friendship, we know so fully
what the other has been doing. Bound to each other
like mountaineers coming down from a mountain,
bound with the tie of the delivery-room,
we wander down the hall to the bathroom, I can
hardly walk, I wobble through the granular
shadowless air, I know where you are
with my eyes closed, we are bound to each other
with huge invisible threads, our sexes
muted, exhausted, crushed, the whole
body a sex – surely this
is the most blessed time of my life,
our children asleep in their beds, each fate
like a vein of abiding mineral
not discovered yet. I sit
on the toilet in the night, you are somewhere in the room,
I open the window and snow has fallen in a
steep drift, against the pane, I
look up, into it,
a wall of cold crystals, silent
and glistening, I quietly call to you
and you come and hold my hand and I say
I cannot see beyond it, I cannot see beyond it.

After Making Love We Hear Footsteps

GALWAY KINNELL
(USA, *b.* 1927)

For I can snore like a bullhorn
or play loud music
or sit up talking with any reasonably sober Irishman
and Fergus will only sink deeper
into his dreamless sleep, which goes by all in one flash,
but let there be that heavy breathing
or a stifled come-cry anywhere in the house
and he will wrench himself awake
and make for it on the run – as now, we lie together,
after making love, quiet, touching along the length of our bodies,
familiar touch of the long-married,
and he appears – in his baseball pajamas, it happens,
the neck opening so small he has to screw them on –
and flops down between us and hugs us and snuggles himself
        to sleep,
his face gleaming with satisfaction at being this very child.

In the half darkness we look at each other
and smile
and touch arms across this little, startlingly muscled body –
this one whom habit of memory propels to the ground of his
        making,
sleeper only the mortal sounds can sing awake,
this blessing love gives again into our arms.

The Flea

JOHN DONNE

(England, 1572-1631)

Mark but this flea, and mark in this,
How little that which thou deny'st me is;
Me it sucked first, and now sucks thee,
And in this flea, our two bloods mingled be;
Confess it, this cannot be said
A sin, or shame, or loss of maidenhead,
    Yet this enjoys before it woo,
    And pampered swells with one blood made of two,
    And this, alas, is more than we would do.

Oh stay, three lives in one flea spare,
Where we almost, nay more than married are.
This flea is you and I, and this
Our marriage bed, and marriage temple is;
Though parents grudge, and you, we'are met,
And cloistered in these living walls of jet.
    Though use make you apt to kill me,
    Let not to that, self-murder added be,
    And sacrilege, three sins in killing three.

Cruel and sudden, hast thou since
Purpled thy nail, in blood of innocence?
In what could this flea guilty be,
Except in that drop which it sucked from thee?
Yet thou triumph'st, and say'st that thou
Find'st not thyself, nor me the weaker now;
    'Tis true, then learn how false, fears be:
    Just so much honour, when thou yield'st to me,
    Will waste, as this flea's death took life from thee.

Wedding

ALICE OSWALD

(England, *b.* 1966)

From time to time our love is like a sail
and when the sail begins to alternate
from tack to tack, it's like a swallowtail
and when the swallow flies it's like a coat;
and if the coat is yours, it has a tear
like a wide mouth and when the mouth begins
to draw the wind, it's like a trumpeter
and when the trumpet blows, it blows like millions
and this, my love, when millions come and go
beyond the need of us, is like a trick;
and when the trick begins, it's like a toe
tiptoeing on a rope, which is like luck;
and when the luck begins, it's like a wedding,
which is like love, which is like everything.

'Let me not to the marriage of true minds'

WILLIAM SHAKESPEARE

(England, 1564-1616)

Let me not to the marriage of true minds
Admit impediments; love is not love
Which alters when it alteration finds,
Or bends with the remover to remove.
O, no, it is an ever-fixèd mark
That looks on tempests and is never shaken;
It is the star to every wand'ring bark,
Whose worth's unknown, although his height be taken.
Love's not Time's fool, though rosy lips and cheeks
Within his bending sickle's compass come;
Love alters not with his brief hours and weeks,
But bears it out even to the edge of doom.
　If this be error and upon me proved,
　I never writ, nor no man ever loved.

'I loved you first…'

CHRISTINA ROSSETTI

(England, 1830-94)

I loved you first: but afterwards your love,
   Outsoaring mine, sang such a loftier song
As drowned the friendly cooings of my dove.
   Which owes the other most? My love was long,
   And yours one moment seemed to wax more strong;
I loved and guessed at you, you construed me
And loved me for what might or might not be –
   Nay, weights and measures do us both a wrong.
For verily love knows not 'mine' or 'thine';
With separate 'I' and 'thou' free love has done,
      For one is both and both are one in love:
Rich love knows nought of 'thine that is not mine';
      Both have the strength and both the length thereof,
   Both of us, of the love which makes us one.

'Oh, no – not even when first we loved...'

THOMAS MOORE

(Ireland, 1779-1852)

Oh, no – not even when first we loved
Wert thou as dear as now thou art;
Thy beauty then my senses moved,
But now my virtues bind my heart.
What was but Passion's sigh before
Has since been turned to Reason's vow;
And, though I then might love thee more,
Trust me, I love thee better now.

Although my heart in earlier youth
Might kindle with more wild desire,
Believe me, it has gained in truth
Much more than it has lost in fire.
The flame now warms my inmost core
That then but sparkled o'er my brow,
And though I seemed to love thee more,
Yet, oh, I love thee better now.

True Ways of Knowing

NORMAN MacCAIG

(Scotland, 1910-96)

Not an ounce excessive, not an inch too little,
Our easy reciprocations. You let me know
The way a boat would feel, if it could feel,
The intimate support of water.

The news you bring me has been news forever,
So that I understand what a stone would say
If only a stone could speak. Is it sad a grassblade
Can't know how it is lovely?

Is it sad that you can't know, except by hearsay
(My gossiping failing words) that you are the way
A water is that can clench its palm and crumple
A boat's confiding timbers?

But that's excessive, and too little. Knowing
The way a circle would describe its roundness,
We touch two selves and feel, complete and gentle,
The intimate support of being.

The way that flight would feel a bird flying
(If it could feel) is the way a space that's in
A stone that's in a water would know itself
If it had our way of knowing.

The Song

(after Rilke)

DANA GIOIA
(USA, *b.* 1950)

version after the German of RAINER MARIA RILKE
(1875-1926)

How shall I hold my soul that it
does not touch yours? How shall I lift
it over you to other things?
If it would only sink below
into the dark like some lost thing
or slumber in some quiet place
which did not echo your soft heart's beat.
But all that ever touched us – you and me –
touched us together
like a bow
that from two strings could draw one voice.
On what instrument were we strung?
And to what player did we sing
our interrupted song?

For What Binds Us

JANE HIRSHFIELD
(USA, *b.* 1953)

There are names for what binds us:
strong forces, weak forces.
Look around, you can see them:
the skin that forms in a half-empty cup,
nails rusting into the places they join,
joints dovetailed on their own weight.
The way things stay so solidly
wherever they've been set down –
and gravity, scientists say, is weak.

And see how the flesh grows back
across a wound, with a great vehemence,
more strong
than the simple, untested surface before.
There's a name for it on horses,
when it comes back darker and raised: proud flesh,

as all flesh
is proud of its wounds, wears them
as honors given out after battle,
small triumphs pinned to the chest –

And when two people have loved each other
see how it is like a
scar between their bodies,
stronger, darker, and proud;
how the black cord makes of them a single fabric
that nothing can tear or mend.

Implications of one plus one

MARGE PIERCY
(USA, *b.* 1936)

Sometimes we collide, tectonic plates merging,
continents shoving, crumpling down into the molten
veins of fire deep in the earth and raising
tons of rock into jagged crests of Sierra.

Sometimes your hands drift on me, milkweed's
airy silk, wingtip's feathery caresses,
our lips grazing, a drift of desires gathering
like fog over warm water, thickening to rain.

Sometimes we go to it heartily, digging,
burrowing, grunting, tossing up covers
like loose earth, nosing into the other's
flesh with hot nozzles and wallowing there.

Sometimes we are kids making out, silly
in the quilt, tickling the xylophone spine,
blowing wet jokes, loud as a whole
slumber party bouncing till the bed breaks.

I go round and round you sometimes, scouting,
blundering, seeking a way in, the high boxwood
maze I penetrate running lungs bursting
toward the fountain of green fire at the heart.

Sometimes you open wide as cathedral doors
and yank me inside. Sometimes you slither
into me like a snake into its burrow.
Sometimes you march in with a brass band.

Ten years of fitting our bodies together
and still they sing wild songs in new keys.
It is more and less than love: timing,
chemistry, magic and will and luck.

One plus one equal one, unknowable except
in the moment, not convertible into words,
not explicable or philosophically interesting.
But it is. And it is. And it is. Amen.

Teodoro Luna's Two Kisses

ALBERTO RÍOS
(USA, *b.* 1952)

Mr Teodoro Luna in his later years had taken to kissing
His wife
Not so much with his lips as with his brows.
This is not to say he put his forehead
Against her mouth –
Rather, he would lift his eyebrows, once quickly:
Not so vigorously he might be confused with the villain
Famous in the theaters, one of accident. This way
He kissed her
Often and quietly, across tables and through doorways,
Sometimes in photographs, and so through the years themselves.
This was his passion, that only she might see. The chance
He might feel some movement on her lips
Toward laughter.

Kissing

FLEUR ADCOCK

(New Zealand / England, *b.* 1934)

The young are walking on the riverbank,
arms around each other's waists and shoulders,
pretending to be looking at the waterlilies
and what might be a nest of some kind, over
there, which two who are clamped together
mouth to mouth have forgotten about.
The others, making courteous detours
around them, talk, stop talking, kiss.
They can see no one older than themselves.
It's their river. They've got all day.

Seeing's not everything. At this very
moment the middle-aged are kissing
in the backs of taxis, on the way
to airports and stations. Their mouths and tongues
are soft and powerful and as moist as ever.
Their hands are not inside each other's clothes
(because of the driver) but locked so tightly
together that it hurts: it may leave marks
on their not of course youthful skin, which they won't
notice. They too may have futures.

And You, Helen

EDWARD THOMAS
(England, 1878-1917)

And you, Helen, what should I give you?
So many things I would give you
Had I an infinite great store
Offered me and I stood before
To choose. I would give you youth,
All kinds of loveliness and truth,
A clear eye as good as mine,
Lands, waters, flowers, wine,
As many children as your heart
Might wish for, a far better art
Than mine can be, all you have lost
Upon the travelling waters tossed,
Or given to me. If I could choose
Freely in that great treasure-house
Anything from any shelf,
I would give you back yourself,
And power to discriminate
What you want and want it not too late,
Many fair days free from care
And heart to enjoy both foul and fair,
And myself, too, if I could find
Where it lay hidden and it proved kind.

Lullaby

W.H. AUDEN
(England, 1907-73)

Lay your sleeping head, my love,
Human on my faithless arm;
Time and fevers burn away
Individual beauty from
Thoughtful children, and the grave
Proves the child ephemeral:
But in my arms till break of day
Let the living creature lie,
Mortal, guilty, but to me
The entirely beautiful.

Soul and body have no bounds:
To lovers as they lie upon
Her tolerant enchanted slope
In their ordinary swoon,
Grave the vision Venus sends
Of supernatural sympathy,
Universal love and hope;
While an abstract insight wakes
Among the glaciers and the rocks
The hermit's sensual ecstasy.

Certainty, fidelity
On the stroke of midnight pass
Like vibrations of a bell,
And fashionable madmen raise
Their pedantic boring cry:
Every farthing of the cost,
All the dreaded cards foretell,
Shall be paid, but from this night
Not a whisper, not a thought,
Not a kiss nor look be lost.

Beauty, midnight, vision dies:
Let the winds of dawn that blow
Softly round your dreaming head
Such a day of sweetness show
Eye and knocking heart may bless,
Find the mortal world enough;
Noons of dryness see you fed
By the involuntary powers,
Nights of insult let you pass
Watched by every human love.

A Valediction: forbidding Mourning

JOHN DONNE

(England, 1572-1631)

As virtuous men pass mildly away,
   And whisper to their souls, to go,
Whilst some of their sad friends do say,
   The breath goes now, and some say, no:

So let us melt, and make no noise,
   No tear-floods, nor sigh-tempests move,
'Twere profanation of our joys
   To tell the laity our love.

Moving of th' earth brings harms and fears,
   Men reckon what it did and meant,
But trepidation of the spheres,
   Though greater far, is innocent.

Dull sublunary lovers' love
   (Whose soul is sense) cannot admit
Absence, because it doth remove
   Those things which elemented it.

But we by a love, so much refined,
   That our selves know not what it is,
Inter-assurèd of the mind,
   Care less, eyes, lips, and hands to miss.

Our two souls therefore, which are one,
   Though I must go, endure not yet
A breach, but an expansion,
   Like gold to aery thinness beat.

If they be two, they are two so
   As stiff twin compasses are two,
Thy soul the fixed foot, makes no show
   To move, but doth, it th'other do.

And though it in the centre sit,
   Yet when the other far doth roam,
It leans, and hearkens after it,
   And grows erect, as that comes home.

Such wilt thou be to me, who must
   Like th' other foot, obliquely run;
Thy firmness makes my circle just,
   And makes me end, where I begun.

Acknowledgements

The poems in this anthology are reprinted from the following books, all by permission of the publishers listed unless stated otherwise. Thanks are due to all the copyright holders cited below for their kind permission:

Fleur Adcock: *Poems 1960-2000* (Bloodaxe Books, 2000). **Kim Addonizio**: ‘For Desire’ and Like That’ from *Tell Me* (BOA Editions, USA, 2000), ‘You Don’t Know What Love Is’ from *What Is This Thing Called Love* (W.W. Norton & Company, 2004). **Yehuda Amichai**: *Selected Poems*, ed. Ted Hughes & Daniel Weissbort (Faber & Faber, 2000). **Marcus Argentarius**: ‘Love is not…’ tr. Fleur Adcock, from *The Greek Anthology and other ancient Greek epigrams*, ed. Peter Jay (Allen Lane, 1973), by permission of the translator. **W.H. Auden**: *Collected Poems*, ed. Edward Mendelson (Faber & Faber, 1991).

John Berryman: *Collected Poems 1937-1971*, ed. Charles Thornbury (Faber & Faber, 1990). **Elizabeth Bishop**: *The Complete Poems 1927-1979* (Chatto & Windus, 1983), by permission of Farrar, Straus & Giroux, Inc.

David Campbell: *Collected Poems*, ed. Leonie Kramer (Angus & Robertson, North Ryde, NSW, Australia, 1989). **Raymond Carver**: *All of Us: Collected Poems* (Harvill Press, 1996), by permission of International Creative Management, Inc., copyright © 1996 Tess Gallagher. **Catullus**: *Poems of Love and Hate*, tr. Josephine Balmer (Bloodaxe Books, 2004). **C.P. Cavafy**: *Collected Poems*, tr. Edmund Keeley & Philip Sherrard (Hogarth Press, 1990), by permission of the estate of C.P. Cavafy and Random House Group Ltd. **David Constantine**: *Collected Poems* (Bloodaxe Books, 2004). **Julia Copus**: *In Defence of Adultery* (Bloodaxe Books, 2003). **E.E. Cummings**: *Complete Poems 1904-1962* (Liveright, 1994), by permission of W.W. Norton & Company, copyright © 1991 by the Trustees for the E.E. Cummings Trust and George James Firmage.

Emily Dickinson: *The Poems of Emily Dickinson*, ed. Ralph W. Franklin (Harvard University Press, 1998). **Michael Donaghy**: *Dances Learned Last Night: Poems 1975-1995* (Picador, 2000), by permission of Macmillan Publishers Ltd. **Carol Ann Duffy**: ‘Warming Her Pearls’ from *Selling Manhattan* (Anvil Press Poetry, 1987), ‘Valentine’ from *Mean Time* (Anvil Press Poetry, 1993). **Helen Dunmore**: *Out of the Blue: Poems 1975-2001* (Bloodaxe Books, 2001). **Paul Durcan**: *A Snail in My Prime: New & Selected Poems* (The Harvill Press, 1993), by permission of the author and Blackstaff Press.

U.A. Fanthorpe: *Safe as Houses* (Peterloo Poets, 1995), reprinted from *Collected Poems* (Peterloo Poets, 2005). **James Fenton**: *Out of Danger* (Penguin Books, 1993), by permission of PFD. **John Fuller**: *Collected Poems* (Chatto & Windus, 1996), by permission of PFD.

Tess Gallagher: *Portable Kisses* (Bloodaxe Books, 1996). **Dana Gioia**: *The Gods of Winter* (Peterloo Poets/Graywolf Press, 1991), by permission of Peterloo Poets. **Jack Gilbert**: *The Great Fires: Poems 1982-1992* (Alfred A. Knopf, NY, 1995). **Nikki Giovanni**: *The Collected Poetry of Nikki Giovanni 1968-1998* (William Morrow, 2003), by permission of the author. **Thom Gunn**: *Collected Poems* (Faber & Faber, 1993).

Marilyn Hacker: *Love, Death, and the Changing of the Seasons* (W.W. Norton & Company, 1995), by permission of MBA Literary Agents Ltd. **Seamus Heaney**: *Opened Ground: Poems 1966-1996* (Faber & Faber, 1998). **Rita Ann Higgins**: *Throw in the Vowels: New & Selected Poems* (Bloodaxe Books, 2005). **Selima Hill**: 'Desire's a Desire' from *A Little Book of Meat* (Bloodaxe Books, 1993), 'Please Can I Have a Man' from *Violet* (Bloodaxe Books, 1997). **Jane Hirshfield**: *Each Happiness Ringed by Lions: Selected Poems* (Bloodaxe Books, 2005).

Elizabeth Jennings: 'Friendship' from *New Collected Poems* (Carcanet Press, 2002), by permission of David Higham Associates.

Jackie Kay: *Life Mask* (Bloodaxe Books, 2005). **Galway Kinnell**: *Selected Poems* (Bloodaxe Books, 2001).

Audre Lorde: *Undersong: Chosen Poems Old and New* (W.W. Norton & Company, 1992; Virago Press, 1993), by permission of Charlotte Sheedy Literary Agency.

James McAuley: *Collected Poems* (Angus & Robertson, Australia, 1980), by permission of HarperCollins Publishers, Australia, and Norma McAuley. **Norman MacCaig**: *The Poems of Norman MacCaig* (Polygon, 2005), by permission of Birlinn Ltd. **Louis MacNeice**: *Collected Poems*, ed. E.R. Dodds (Faber, 1979), by permission of David Higham Associates Ltd. **Michelangelo**: 'If love is chaste…', tr. Elizabeth Jennings, from *The Sonnets of Michelangelo* (Carcanet Press, 2003), translated by Elizabeth Jennings, by permission of David Higham Associates. **Edwin Muir**: *Collected Poems* (Faber & Faber, 1963).

Pablo Neruda: 'I crave your mouth, your voice, your hair' from *100 Love Sonnets/Cien sonetos de amor*, tr. Stephen Tapscott (University of Texas Press, 1986); 'I don't love you as if you were the salt-rose, topaz' from *Full Woman, Fleshly Apple, Hot Moon,* tr. Stephen Mitchell (HarperCollins, NY, 1997). **Grace Nichols**: *The Fat Black Woman's Poems* (Virago Press, 1984), by permission of Curtis Brown Ltd.

Sharon Olds: *Strike Sparks: Selected Poems 1980-2002* (Alfred A. Knopf, Inc, 2004; Jonathan Cape, 2005), by permission of the Random House Group Ltd and Alfred A. Knopf, division of Random House, Inc. **Michael Ondaatje**: *The Cinnamon Peeler: Selected Poems* (Picador, 1989), by permission of the Ellen Levine Literary Agency, Inc. **Alice Oswald**: *The Thing in the Gap-Stone Stile* (Oxford University Press, 1996), by permission of PFD and the author.

Marge Piercy: 'Raisin pumpernickel' from *Available Light* (Knopf, New York, 1988), 'Implications of one plus one' from *Eight Chambers of the Heart: Selected Poems* (Penguin Books, 1995), by permission of The Wallace Literary Agency, Inc.

Alberto Ríos: *Teodoro Luna's Two Kisses: poems* (W.W. Norton & Company, 1990). **Rumi**: *The Essential Rumi,* tr. Coleman Barks & John Mayne, (HarperCollins, USA, 1995; Penguin Books, 1999), © Coleman Barks, also by permission of the Reid Boates Literary Agency.

Sappho: *Poems & Fragments*, trs. Josephine Balmer (Bloodaxe Books, 1992). **Anne Sexton**: *Complete Poems*, ed. Maxine Kumin (Mariner Books, USA, 1999), by permission of Sterling Lord Literistic, Inc. **Jo Shapcott**: *Her Book: Poems 1988-1998* (Faber & Faber, 2000). **Stevie Smith**: *Collected Poems*, ed. James MacGibbon (Penguin, 1985), by permission of the James MacGibbon Estate. **William Jay Smith**: *The World Below the Window: Poems, 1937-1997* (Johns Hopkins University Press, 1998).

Fyodor Tyutchev: 'Last Love', translated by Vladimir Nabokov, by permission of the Estate of Vladimir Nabokov, © Dmitri Nabokov.

W.B. Yeats: *The Poems*, ed. Richard J. Finneran (Macmillan, 1991), by permission of A.P. Watt Ltd on behalf of Michael B. Yeats.

Every effort has been made to trace copyright holders of the poems published in this book. We apologise if any material has been included without permission or without the appropriate acknowledgement, and would be glad to be told of anyone who has not been consulted.

I would like to thank Pamela Robertson-Pearce for her love and support, which made the making of this book such a pleasure, as well as for suggesting its title and some of the poems.